Read-About® Science

What Is Velocity?

By Joanne Barkan

Consultant
Linda Bullock
Science Curriculum Specialist

Children's Press®
A Division of Scholastic Inc.
New York   Toronto   London   Auckland   Sydney
Mexico City   New Delhi   Hong Kong
Danbury, Connecticut

Designer: Herman Adler Design
Photo Researcher: Caroline Anderson
The photo on the cover shows a boy riding his bicycle.

Library of Congress Cataloging-in-Publication Data

Barkan, Joanne.
  What is velocity? / by Joanne Barkan ; consultant, Linda Bullock.
    p. cm. — (Rookie read-about science)
  Includes index.
  ISBN 0-516-23616-4 (lib. bdg.)   0-516-24664-X (pbk.)
  1. Velocity—Juvenile literature. I. Title. II. Series.
  QC137.52.B37 2004
  531'.112—dc22

                  2004001225

CHILDREN'S PRESS, and ROOKIE READ-ABOUT®,
and associated logos are trademarks and or registered trademarks
of Scholastic Library Publishing. SCHOLASTIC and associated logos
are trademarks and or registered trademarks of Scholastic Inc.

1 2 3 4 5 6 7 8 9 10 R 13 12 11 10 09 08 07 06 05 04

Oh, no! You are going to
be late for school!

Hurry! You can get to school in five minutes instead of ten.

How? Walk faster. Pick up your speed.

Speed tells us how fast something moves. An airplane moves at a high speed.

A snail moves at a low speed.

You can measure speed. You can find out how far something or someone moves in a certain time.

This rider travels one block in one minute.

This car goes fifty miles in one hour.

This girl runs thirty yards
in ten seconds.

14

Earth moves around the sun in one year.

A speedometer is a tool that measures speed. Cars have speedometers. Some bikes have them, too.

This rider checks his speedometer. He is hurrying to a baseball game.

Speedometer

The pitcher throws the ball hard. It whizzes through the air.

The ball reaches the batter. Crack! It's a hit!

You know two things
about the ball.

First, the pitcher threw
the ball to the batter. This
was the ball's direction
(duh-RECK-shun).

Second, the ball's speed
was fast.

Speed plus direction tell you the ball's velocity (vuh-LOSS-uh-tee).

Everything that moves has velocity.

23

This train has velocity.
It travels 200 miles in one
hour. It is headed north.

The train's velocity is 200
miles per hour north.

The train picks up speed. Now it is going 250 miles per hour north. Its velocity has changed.

The train changes direction. Now it is going 250 miles per hour west. Its velocity has changed again.

This toy has velocity, too.

How far does it go?
How long does it take?
What direction is it going?

Answer these questions
and you will know the
toy's velocity.

Words You Know

airplane

direction

snail

speedometer

train

Index

About the Author

Joanne Barkan is a science writer. Her book about fireflies and other creatures that glow has won awards from the National Science Teachers' Association, the Children's Book Council, and Parents' Choice. Joanne makes her home in both New York City and Cape Cod.

Photo Credits

Photographs © 2004: Dwight R. Kuhn Photography: 7, 31 top left; Ellen B. Senisi: cover, 5, 29; Nance S. Trueworthy: 10, 17, 31 top right; Peter Arnold Inc.: 6, 30 top (David J. Cross), 24, 27, 31 bottom (P. Frischmuth/Argus Fotoarchiv); Photo Researchers, NY: 9 (Tim Davis), 14 (David Hardy/SPL); PhotoEdit: 3 (Tony Freeman), 23 (Dennis MacDonald); The Image Works: 13 (Bob Daemmrich), 20, 30 bottom (Peter Hvizdak), 19 (Jacksonville Journal Courier).